THE GLASS
OF WATER

THE GLASS OF WATER

How far would you go to refresh your leader?

ANDY ELMES

to be done that you could assist him with. These are a just a few things to get you thinking. Hopefully this gives you insight and opens your heart to something you may have not realised before. Now that you have become aware of the situation, you probably do know your leader well enough to know when they need something and what it is that they need. As you act upon this, you will find that this is actually very good wisdom for protecting the longevity of the success of your church. Think about it, if the goose is well taken care of, then it can keep on producing the golden eggs so that the church can keep on producing golden omelettes! Everyone is happy. The Bible uses this same principle but instead of using a goose as the example, it speaks of an ox:

> For it is written in the Law of Moses: 'Do not muzzle an ox while it is treading out the grain.' Is it about oxen that God is concerned? Surely he says this for us, doesn't he? Yes, this was written for us, because whoever ploughs and threshes should be able to do so in the hope of sharing in the harvest. (1 Corinthians 9:9-10)

Here the Apostle Paul is basically defending his right and the right of those who minister the Word to be taken care of by the people who are being ministered to. If you read the verse in context you will see this is exactly the point he is trying to make. I would like to pick up on the analogy he uses from the Law of Moses, as he highlights the principle that says 'do not muzzle the ox while it is treading out the grain'. What is he saying here? I believe it's the same thing I am saying throughout this book! As a mighty man to your leader, make sure that you are freeing them from the things that get in the way of what they do best. Make sure they are not being 'muzzled', whether it be in their finances, their time or their freedom to move as God directs them. It becomes simply a matter of helping them practically, to make sure that they are free to do what God has called them to do, free to think about what they need to think about, free to lead like they need to lead. And, if you are in leadership with them, to make doubly sure you are not unknowingly a part of the very muzzle that is restricting them!

I anticipate a number of different initial reactions from people when they read this chapter – everything from realisation to total offence. Let me just underline and clarify what I am *not* saying for those who may be on the side of becoming offended. I am not saying to worship or idolise your pastor or treat them like some pope-like figure who can do no wrong. I am simply saying treat them as a gift God has given you, not taking them for granted. They may have answered a call of God to serve in ministry, but that doesn't mean it did not come without great personal sacrifice. They counted the cost and put the advancement of the kingdom of God before their own needs or desires. Many a man or woman of God has given up material success or promising futures in order to serve in a ministry where they are expected to give all with little gratitude or return. However, on the opposite end of the spectrum, I have seen the way religion exalts certain humans, bringing them to unhealthy places of adoration and 'celebrity' status. I, too, am disgusted and confused as to why people would do this. But, equally, I am amazed at how churches choose to treat the leaders God has given them, overlooking the everyday needs of their 'David' and actually hiding behind religious mindsets and quietly thinking insultingly demeaning things like, 'it's our job to keep them poor so God can keep them humble'. We need to find a point of godly balance on this issue! A place of reality that does not create a senior leader to be worshipped and idolised, but equally does not leave them and their family lacking, under cared for, weary of battle and ready to quit.

This, I believe, is the role of mighty men, and they are the ones that set the culture around the leader, who love them for who they are as much as what they do. Hold your sword until it fuses to your hand, and defend that lentil field from the enemy. But at the same time, be watching David's face, be looking for what they and their family need to keep doing what God has appointed them to do. This is what makes a mighty man. Is that who you are? As you have hopefully seen there is a significant difference between being one of David's army and being one of David's mighty men. Although they both seem to do the same and even produce the same, the latter one carries with it a greater awareness and love for the leader as a person. Which one do you really want to be? If being in David's army is enough for you then do it with all your might. If being a mighty man to your David is your heart's desire then step up above the crowd and be that person.

I know that by now I have provoked all manner of thoughts concerning how you can be a 'mighty man' to the leader God has given you. Please take quality time to process these thoughts and ask yourselves and your team the honest questions that need to be asked. The following questions will reveal a number of things about your heart towards them. Take time to listen to your response.

Thought provokers:

* Are you a mighty man or just a leader?

* Do your exploits separate you from others in the team?

* Do you notice what your leader needs or do you just applaud what they produce?

* What can you do to help them keep 'laying eggs' and 'treading the grain'?

* Are you looking for ways to refresh your leader so they won't become a negative statistic?

* What would a glass of water look like for your leader? Is there something you could do that would meet that need?

Footnotes

1. *Statistics on Pastors*, by Dr Richard J. Krejcir (2007, research from 1989 to 2006); http://www.intothyword.org/apps/articles/default.asp?articleid=36562&content

2. *Don't Make Your Pastor a Statistic*, by Thabiti Anyabwile (2011); http://www.9marks.org/blog/dont-make-your-pastor-statistic

3. *Aesop's Fables*, a new translation by V. S. Vernon Jones (London: W. Heinemann, 1912), p. 2.

Understanding their world

ANDY ELMES

2

'**B**ut they are just like us, we all go through the same things in life don't we?' My answer to this type of question is very blunt – No, we don't. A pastor may put their clothes on like any other person, but things are certainly not the same for them, of this I can assure you. Let me explain this a little bit further and give you some interesting insight into the world of a visionary or senior leader. How am I qualified to give you such a detailed, concise tour into this inner world of senior leader? Because I am one.

To fully acquire a heart to be an effective mighty man for your leader, you need to have an understanding of what their world is actually like, rather than what you might imagine it to be. As I have said before, most people in churches today would honestly think we are all the same and that a pastor doesn't deal with anything more than anyone of us. Let me give you some insight as to why this thought process is far from true. Please allow me to be your bus driver on this tour, someone who dares to take you on a journey to the real daily world of your leader. Buckle up, this could be an interesting ride and you may be in for some surprises.

Two dimensional pressures

The first reality that must be grasped is that your leader has to deal with a two dimensional pressure on their life.

By this I mean they have two very different types of pressure coming from two very different realms, while the normal everyday guy would usually have to deal with one.

The pressures of life

Life's pressures are what we all have in common, the ones that indeed make the leader just like anyone else. Bills to pay, kids to raise, homes to keep, marriages to steward, cars to repair, transport to schools each day and the list could go on and on. The average non-celebrity senior leader experiences all of these things like any other person does. They, too, strive to balance budgets, make money stretch and try to tell their kids why they can't have everything that's advertised on TV! They get toothaches and have washing machines that stop working when you need them most. Yep, you're right, in this context, they're just like everyone else living a normal life that's full of daily trials and stresses. But what you may not realise is at the same time they are experiencing another very real dimension of continuous onslaught. This is what I refer to as spiritual pressure.

Spiritual pressure

So let us try to unpack this one carefully, because it's important that you don't misunderstand. Let me explain that I am aware that every believer faces a measurement of spiritual pressure, which is in direct accordance with what they have been called to do for the Lord. Nevertheless,

So, you clearly see the twelve Apostles, the men who Jesus originally anointed to lead the church, leading very successfully. As the church rapidly grew, it created some practical problems that were now affecting the successful running of the church. Some management decisions had to be made to ensure that the spiritual leaders did not have to 'abandon their responsibilities' in order to take care of the needs their own ministry was creating through that growth. A business meeting was called, and the elders chose trusted people to be appointed. Then the leaders laid hands on them to empower (anoint) them to do the work of the ministry, which was to help run the church. Thus, the first committee was established in the early church. Most of you know that this is where the role of the church deacon originally came from. This position was one of being a 'super servant', helping the church to continue to run in an effective way. These were people who loved to serve and take care of what needed to be done to keep the church healthy, moving and growing. Anointed and commissioned for the task, they were eldership-appointed servants who never strived for position, but rather found fulfilment in making God's house the best it could be.

So what has happened today? I have visited some churches where the chain of command is so out of balance it is amazing. I have seen pastors who are being negatively controlled, limited and held back by their deacons and boards, instead of empowered and refreshed and released by them. I have seen what has been termed 'deacon-possessed' churches, in which the board thinks they are in charge and the senior leader is their puppet to execute their orders. Sorry to offend, but I don't see that type of church government in the New Testament. Like I said, I may be a bit old school in my view point but I believe that God anoints a leader who leads the church with elders who then appoint the right people to help run the church successfully, legally and proficiently. The senior leader should never be made to feel like a puppet on a string but, rather, he should be empowered and refreshed by the support of those who provide godly, practical wisdom and encouragement. Church leadership should serve as the protector of its leader, not strive to keep him humble or keep him 'grounded'. That is the role of the God-given apostles and peer friendships in his life. Let the visionary have his vision! Don't stifle it or try to impose negativity to put out the dream. Every great work of God began with a step of faith. A wise deacon or trustee knows how to allow the leader to have his vision, while still able to guide and advise. Once again, let me clarify that directors, trustees and business-minded boards carry a very important role within every church, yet they do not spiritually lead the church. They exist to serve the spiritual leader and their eldership, to monitor that everything is done legally according to the law of the land. They are also there to offer wisdom to help the church leadership make the best decisions they can, providing them with the relevant information they need to make those decisions. This flows from a 'same team' heart, with all wanting to see the godly vision on the leader's heart fulfilled, while also morally and legally protecting the leader, his family and primarily the church.

I believe we again see these realities in the ministry of Jesus, who should always be our role model and blueprint:

*He **appointed** twelve that they might be with him and that he might send them out to preach. (Mark 3:14)*

*After this the LORD **appointed** seventy-two others and sent them two by two ahead of him to every town and place where he was about to go. (Luke 10:1)*

We also see this model operating in the life of the first church as it expanded across the earth:

*Paul and Barnabas **appointed** elders for them in each church and, with prayer and fasting, committed them to the LORD, in whom they had put their trust. (Acts 14:23)*

Many other verses show this to be the method of the early church and it worked. Men who were anointed elders would appoint leaders and establish strong local churches that flowed under an apostolic anointing. How we work that out today may vary slightly, but I do not believe that we should move away from the blueprint for leadership that God set in place. Yes, there should be accountability. Yes, things must be done with wisdom, strategy and input from people who are experts in their field. But I don't believe that the anointing on the set man (visionary leader) and his eldership should be *controlled* by 'appointed' leadership.

Be very careful what you touch

'Do not touch my anointed ones; do my prophets no harm.'
(Psalm 105:15)

This is again one of those 'hot potato' verses that has been greatly misunderstood and even abused over the years by people who never fully understood it, or used it to lead in a manipulative or dictatorial way. Yet we cannot afford to be those who 'throw the baby out with the bathwater'. We need to understand what God is saying to us in this verse. When you want to understand what the anointing is and how to treat it correctly, I believe there is no greater example than David. When you study the life of King David you see he had a great personal ethic and a clear revelation of the sanctity of the anointing. He knew the importance of honouring it on the life of another, even if that other was trying to kill him and do him harm on a daily basis.

Though he himself had been called and anointed by God to lead Israel and take over the kingdom from Saul (1 Samuel 16:13), there was a time when David served under him, while Saul was still the king. David knew he had been called, but also had to trust God with how the exchange was going to take place. In all this he knew that there was still a God-given anointing in place on Saul's life. Because of this, he took a personal stand, keeping a healthy fear not to touch that anointing, even when his mighty men were constantly encouraging him to take advantage of opportunities to do so.

As the story is told in the Old Testament, Saul was pursuing David because he already had a sense of David's future leadership as evidenced by the favour he had with the people. This irritated him to his core and, though he genuinely loved David, he hated him as well. This caused some really bizarre encounters that finally forced David to flee. A couple of times while Saul was in pursuit of him, he unknowingly camped so close to David and his men that David actually had the opportunity to creep into his camp by night and do him great harm. More than once David had the chance to kill Saul and bring his own reign into being. But something in him could not touch Saul. Why? Because he knew God's anointing was still on him; and it was his respect and honour for the anointing that made him not want to touch the life of Saul in a bad or harmful way.

The men said, 'This is the day the LORD spoke of when he said to you, "I will give your enemy into your hands for you to deal with as you wish."' Then David crept up unnoticed and cut off a corner of Saul's robe. Afterward, David was conscience-stricken for having cut off a corner of his robe. He said to his men, 'The LORD forbid that I should do such a thing to my master, the LORD's anointed, or lay my hand on him; for he is the anointed of the LORD.' With these words David sharply

*rebuked his men and did not allow them to attack Saul. And
Saul left the cave and went his way. (1 Samuel 24:4-7)*

Here we see when David did get caught up in the moment
of opportunity and boldly cut a corner off Saul's robe. He
almost seems to be contemplating doing what his mighty
men advised him (through Scripture, no less!), but as soon
as his own conscience kicked in, he did what he needed to
do to make recompense for his actions. Another time,
David was in a position where he could easily kill Saul, and
again to his men it seemed a great opportunity and very
much deserved. David chose not to, but rather used the
moment to show Saul that he was honouring the anointing
placed on him through God by not touching him.

*So David and Abishai went to the army by night, and there
was Saul, lying asleep inside the camp with his spear stuck in
the ground near his head. Abner and the soldiers were lying
around him. Abishai said to David, 'Today God has delivered
your enemy into your hands. Now let me pin him to the ground
with one thrust of the spear; I won't strike him twice.' But
David said to Abishai, 'Don't destroy him! Who can lay a
hand on the LORD's anointed and be guiltless? As surely as
the LORD lives,' he said, 'the LORD himself will strike him, or
his time will come and he will die, or he will go into battle
and perish. But the LORD forbid that I should lay a hand on
the LORD's anointed. Now get the spear and water jug that
are near his head, and let's go.' So David took the spear and
water jug near Saul's head, and they left. No one saw or knew*

to be able to use most of their mind power for the benefit of the kingdom? If you could help them get a lot of that other stuff off or out of their mind, how much more of their mind could they give to the church and its future?

It's not that they don't want to give anymore; it's because they can't. How can you help them to get their mind free? What can you do to liberate your leader so they can give the best of the capacity of their mind to leading your church into a new and bigger future? Using an example we've discussed already, how can you further un-muzzle your ox so they can tread more grain for the church? What can you do to help them free up more valuable brain space so they can think church-related things with more available capacity? Once again, you refresh them in doing this and the reward belongs to the future of your church. If they've achieved what they have with what they had spare, what could they achieve if they had more?

God notices

Why, anyone by just giving you a cup of water in my name is on our side. Count on it that God will notice. (Mark 9:41, The Message)

Let me conclude with this. How you treat your leader will be noticed by God. If He gave them to you as a gift, the question really is, how are you treating the gift? Count on it – God will notice. As you honour them, you honour God and He will honour you.

Let me say this one more time: honour is a fading quality and commodity in this world and society we live in. We need to be those who stand up for it. If your leader has been walking with you a number of years ask yourself some simple and real questions:

- Where would you be now if they had not stepped forward to be a leader in your life?

- Where would your family be now? Are they going on with God? If so, would they be if they had not been under this leadership?

- Where would your church be now?

- If this person has been such a blessing to your world, imagine if they are refreshed to keep on going and never quit, how many other people can they help? How many other families can their life make a difference in?

The world teaches you don't know what you've got till it's gone. May this not be your experience; may you realise the gift you actually have in your leader before they've given up, walked away or died. I think we need to re-write this proverb to say, know what you have while you have them, and appreciate and honour them while you can. Live to be that agent of refreshing in their world.

Thought provokers:

* Do you believe a church leader should be well paid and taken care of?

* How well do you feel your leader should be paid? What other job do you feel their calling is comparable to? Is that actually reasonable and godly?

* What practical tasks or responsibilities could you lift off your leader's life to free them up to lead better?

* Can you tell when your leader is caught in a cycle of tough stuff?

* Do you know what your leader likes to do to have fun and be refreshed?

* What would be the main obstacle or 'other thing' that is taking away the full capacity of your leader's mind?

ANDY ELMES

Practical suggestions for serving your leaders better

7

I hope this simple book encourages and inspires you to continue to be the mighty man your leader needs you to be. In this final chapter, I want to give you some very practical tips and suggestions on how to be a blessing and refreshing in the lives of your leaders. I know that each church will have various degrees of ability when it comes to resources, so keep in mind most of what I will share does not cost much financially; just the time, love and energy of people. Also, as I go through different ideas, I am aware that some churches may have great human resources while others may be limited. While they may not be able to do what they really desire to, again I believe if the heart is there, there is potential here for everyone.

As you read through these suggestions, take what works, adapt what you can and plan to do others when you are more able. The main thing is that you don't feel obliged to do something but, rather, inspired to do something based on revelation. As I share on these different ways to be a refreshing to your leader, my insight comes not only from my own life and time in leadership but also other pastors as well. I took the time to ask a number of different church leaders from various denominations the simple question we began this book with: 'If you could tell your leaders to do something for you, or to serve you better, what would